Pieces, Paces, Prayers and Poems

Dory Williams and Dustin Pickering

Transcendent Zero Press

Houston, Texas

ISBN-13: 978-1-946460-36-3
Library of Congress Control Number: 2021925508

Printed in the United States of America

Transcendent Zero Press
16429 El Camino Real Apt. #7
Houston, TX 77062

FIRST EDITION

Pieces, Paces, Prayers and Poems

Dory Williams and Dustin Pickering

Transcendent Zero Press

Houston, Texas

Dory Williams

Close

You held my heart in your hands and it didn't break, but it may. You are a better person than me, modest, not a boaster. If I could just read between the lines and get closer, to what you say.......Let me hold your hand when you pray!

No Proof?

There is no proof because we need God more than He needs us.

Make Life Longer

I can do anything my Loved ones support. That is where I feel strong. Life is too short until It is too long. Too long with struggles of memories of them that haunt. And too short to not do what I want.

Respect for Love

'Reach for the highest possible' is what we've prayed and taught. Love should be above our pay grade. But it's not.

Pride In Between

The only thing standing between you and tragedy is you feeling proud of yourself.

Hanging Your Head

Your eyes go through me. They are so brown. You are frustrated with me so I hang my head down. I think about you like I have something to prove. You left me little clues. But when you disapprove, I look at my shoes. "I love you," say the Fates, not every now and then, but now! When you look down on me, my hardship culminates and I bow.

Close Enough

You say, "I Love you, Babe, " is the line you sell. But do you mean it deep inside, what you say so well? I guess I won't be close enough to tell! Those lines you use on women, I guess I should warn them. And those lies you tell yourself, I'm not sure I'm close enough to scorn them. So I'll just assume Love from you is a bluff. But I must confess, when you're away, you can't be close enough.

Milking Love

There are people who will tell you your dream is a dead end before you start. There are people who say you're not together whenever you are apart. There are people who will break your heart. But the people you know Love you give you the world and say, "Go forth!" Always milk that for whatever it's worth!

Karma

I insulted you so they insulted me and then someone insults them, insulted with what nerve! And if we care, we get what we deserve. Them, you and I. The bible says, "An eye for an eye!" The world spins round like the circles in which we used to hang. I was so vulnerable with you, before we knew what it was to sin, my Life, you could sink your teeth in, where later you showed your fang, ferociously as I stood peacefully, because what I do comes back to me.

She would hang on your arm like a drape, but used you as her way to escape from the fairy tales that make us all a fool. As I sit with my dream of you, to be held and upheld, reaching up and reaching out your hand so I'll stand. In my mind, you represent all of mankind, until I am in hearts and arms of men.......and finally, there'll be Karma again!

The Darkness, Getting Your Mind Off It

You faced that cold feeling that numbs you, and tried to stand up to that darkness that overcomes you. But they don't know what you go through since, your whole Life, you've been focused on you. So how do you get out of your darkness? Without a dream, real Life mars , as you age, and thoughts are bars when the mind's a cage. And, if on your mind is nothing, then the focus is to get your mind off something. To me, an open heart and an open mind are a steeple. The light comes free from thinking of other people.

Your Love's Importance

Maybe how you regard my Love, for you, depends on how I measure up. And often Times, my self Love and fear….. they can disrupt, my Love for you and my value too, those Times I have to see Love through…..I bet in Heaven, when you Love someone, everyone says, "Go forth!" But the world determines my Love's importance right here, on Earth. So I Love you, Dear, in this world, for whatever it's worth.

Imaginary Heart

I wondered and wondered about my bad luck with men. My heart was wild but they silenced me to be tame. Every one of them, the same. But I look inside you to mysteries that change to me. And you are different and strange to me, those inner feelings that vary to me. You are almost imaginary to me! A struggle facing Life on our own, so much time alone. But if you Love me, we won't be apart anymore. You see, I haven't Loved anyone with a heart before.

Still Here

Right now I am a culmination of where I've been, And maybe I never had a chance to win, that fairy tale of hers and his, But that's not all there is! Those boys broke my heart over and over until there is no cure. Then someone said, "You may not win, but you show that you are tougher than you thought you were! Why? Because you're still here!" And that is all I needed to hear.

Relying on a World Wide Dream

Your dream got you through strife with only a little fuss. If something saved your Life, don't you think it is Good enough to share with the rest of us?

Teacher

One old man
Idealistic like a child
Yet strong enough to carry generations.
You know your eyes are stars of hope
We should all find at the bottom of our
Own hearts.
But ours surrounded dark by lies and
lack of knowledge.
With your words you change the
World, and with ours, our world
Still remains hidden.
But maybe you have sparked a hope
Without shame or fear that can
Draw from our hopes so far
Away and yet so near.
And your own will always
Live around you: Not hearing
From us, "Yes, but what can I do?"

White Wings

But you forgot me White Wings.
Left frozen pulls and nothing-stings
Where blue through high green waves of grass.
From this imprisoned, four-wheeled field I pass.
And I knew you well
Just like this noble soul I sell.
Soar loose—till—oops,
I guess you fell.

But it was worth it though, that you got
To fly up high in your paradise lot
Till BOOM!
That pea-brain got you shot.
Pushed from the sky like a sliding rock
Tinkling down a rainbow spiral.
I see You slip. You weren't my rival.
And when you hit my ugly ground
I knew too soon I would fall down
and heavy walk all around.
All on your grave of nothing sounds.
For you, you left me here again to sin again.

Again I sin, I sin.

Certified

Well, what do I know?
Don't tell me "nothing."
It hurts my pride.
My helplessness is long and wide.
My brilliancy so hard to hide.

All the time that I devote,
To all the fate I wrote
Which underlying godly brains
Will glue these labels that I've gained.
You see all these lies just so devised
Can make me modest as well as wise.

I've worked hard to suppress gaps
In my chest and stretch the rest,
Until my head is bigger than yours.
So, for the respect that I do deserve
Can you answer me one question?

If you can't, I'll guess then.
Unknown to me alone, but still,
You might have learned it on a whim.
Can you tell me who I am?

Suffer

All the Gods told me not to smoke—
cause they could not—
cause they were right
So I suffer

All the women told me I thought
Too much like a man
Cause they were scared to think
So I suffer

Someone told me I was ugly
Cause he did not like my mirror—
And called me vain
Before he knew I was ugly
So I suffer

They saw me trying to
Be happy past my suffering
But they will not suffer
So they hated my happiness
So I suffer

And when did they laugh
With you?
You remember?
You made fun of yourself
They used to laugh with you,
Now
You just suffer.

And Shakespeare made us
All suffer
All suffer
So I suffer
Juliet, so we suffer

Out of Control

Time—I own you!
Until You laugh!
Laugh at my past and
Swoop by these sins then

Stand still again
Again I sin. You
Laugh last, laugh last, laugh last again.

And Fate you can't hurt me again.
Time's hostage won't be set free
Stand still, stand still, stand still in me.

Like those burning words still in me
I'll stop you both even if you won't stop.
I know I own you both too well.
Cage me and I'll pull you in my cell with me.
Molding my life.

Fate's rest I know you best
When all of my time is what I test because
Since our love's been sold for a certainty.
My life's been caged by a certitude.

Reason

With all your understanding, you can't wrap your head around things that happen for no reason. They leave you without a trace and left you feeling out of place, in a world where your brains probe and prod, in a world where luck defines God. So I hope for a place where we are better equipped, after luck ruined all I worshipped. A place to bear my soul without fuss, where Love of humanity started with us...... for a reason.

Without a Thought for Myself

When I was young, I only thought of myself, but that was just an inkling of me. All that Time left still thinking of me! Then people scold and say, "Think of others and behave yourself!" So you think of others just to save yourself. But I didn't get the point! I care for them when they won't, and they think of me because I don't. The nourishment of Love, that they need me, is how they feed me. Dependent on Love, yet still independent, is how I send it, is why we've prayed (and we've knelt), until I am never feeding myself.

Flawless

You're not stupid with the Life you've made. You love a "someone" because you know looks will fade. You want to show you're courageous after women pain you, so you go after brains too. In the end you chase the best of the best who put to shame all the rest, and that is where you start. But what about your heart? Because being too concerned by what others think can be a fetter. She may be the best right now but there'll always be someone better!

Give Him A Chance

I cherish the Love I own. You make a move and I swoon. But I'm destined to be alone, everyday that you hang the moon. So I'll accept my Fate (I just won't accept too soon!!).

The Dream Coming True

Them not being able to see your dream coming True left you confused and stumped. They said all those possibilities were lies. But even as you jumped, to you, your dream coming True was still no big surprise.

Alone?

The only way you can be alone is if you stop listening to yourself.

Important Comes From Them

When they are harsh with me because it's important, I realize that I'm important. "You are important, so we are strict" is what they've said. And it is all not just coming from my head.

More Serious Than That

Anyone who thinks life and death is a contest of winning or losing won't win.

Feeling the Real Feelings

When I lie, my eyes get beadier.
And when I'm only thinking of me, and my inadequacies, I get needier.
But then, when I think of you, every thought is lighter and breezier. If you focus on what's important, the hard stuff gets easier.

Needy of the Mysterious

Don't ask to get what you want! Ask to get what God thinks you should want!

Heaven's Near

I got over him because I met you. He hurt me where my feelings were True. You helped me and I left him, even though he knew all the angles. I may not be in Heaven, but I know some people are angels.

Love Survives

You flaunted your strength to not love me. And I was meek to Love you still (for whatever that was worth!). "Only the strong shall survive", but "The meek shall inherit the earth"!

Overestimating Herself

Men have spoiled you and you are used to getting your way. And with the competition, no one ever gets in your way. You meet men by your rule; Eat, Drink and be Merry. But he is married!! He is as vulnerable as the next guy whenever the mood does strike him. But he is not automatically yours just because you like him.

Acknowledging the Weight of the World

"The weight of the world is on everyone's shoulder" is why he loved another. That is what he told her. She says, "Then do your part. The world isn't safe until everyone has a heart!". He tries to keep up with her, since he Loves their abode, where he learned a Love's story. He feels the guilt now instead of the glory, and says to her, "I know you've carried the load for me. You save the world because you adore me". In the end she had to let him go as her world came crashing down, with little fuss. She still does her part because the world is all of us, plus what we do on our own, since you can't save the world with Love alone!

The Sad World

Nature, at Times, shows us her beauty. Like us, it's her job and sense of duty. And it is up to you if you Love or hate her. Nature holds no anger toward you if you don't appreciate her. Beauty made for you, may be by an anointment. If you don't appreciate her, there is no grudge. Just disappointment.

Doing Useful, Not Evil

I choose to do what I have a use for. And I hope I never do what there is no excuse for. Just like everyone who works, wherever evil lurks, I am susceptible. I know I didn't do real harm if I didn't do anything irreparable.

All Their Warnings

They warned me that, "money is the root of all evil", but that luck turns on a dime. They say, about my cream, "don't waste your Time!", before I know what mood a penny brings. Humanity has many ties. You tell me my course of action is unwise, so you apprise.
I am like everyone else who carries regret, though, those mistakes, I don't fret! After they disrupt. Even after you gave me a heads up! But who

would undo many things?? The bottom line is though, that if I had heeded all their warnings, I wouldn't have done anything.

Protect Yourself

There is no greater protection a man can give you then your Love for him.

A Reverie

Those people who don't believe in me left me ignored (is where they lurk). But this dream isn't about me. It's about the work. And they say, "No! A rejection isn't about your hope. It is about you".
Where a hope for happiness is strong, what else about me then is wrong? When a reward is overdue?
A chance might show them who I could be, the old and the new. Then they say, "It's not about your reverie. It's all about you".
My Love of Life and men is a reverie that is not what it seems. How can they say there is so much fault with me when all of me is in my dreams?

A Vision of Where I Go

When I chased True Love, boy! Did I have nerve! (to get there). And then I ran from everything I deserved to anywhere. Mind over matter means there is still a place for us somewhere. You said you didn't Love me, but, from the corner of my eye, I caught your stare. Besides, people change out of nowhere. So, if I can't make someone Love me again, where then? A vision of where I go.
Your eyes on me and Life can't get any clearer. My eyes catch your stare as I look in a mirror. The future of a dream they say was far fetched, in my mind, your portrait etched, and a vision is all I'm thinking of. I can see my Love.

When I'm near you, I am worthy and I pine. I Love you earthly and Divine….. A hopeful mate from a fallen star. But by Fate, I also Love you from afar. Like a vision of where I go.

The Shortage in Her Life

She saw him and he stared at her. In her life, there is a shortage of men of character, because he treated her crudely. He was uncouth. In all our Lives, there is a shortage of Truth, for us, which makes it harder to trust. In her Life, there is a shortage of Love, for example. But people willing to be her friend are ample.

Eternity In A Minute

Thinking sometimes is a feeling underlying. I found your face and my brain found a thought where I wasn't even trying. And there was a minute there where I wasn't even dying. My eyes are a well. You are the water, and my heart is in it. Yet in this test for survival, I may be inferior because I've learned that dreaming doesn't make me superior. How do I win it? So I go to you because that's where I wasn't dying for a minute.

Faith's Way

You chase a dream. It's the only thing you've sought anyway. But don't worry when you run out of steam! All you've got will go a long way.

Where I Live

In Life, sometimes, I feel I'm not part of a team. I sit on the benches and cheer them on, And I know one day, my support will be gone. But I Lived as a team fan. I can't find anyone with more integrity or higher ideals than my dream man. And nothing can take care of me more than my dream can.
My Life is here on the bench. But when we win, you'll have to peel me off the ceiling on this dome…..Living to cheer on others more like a fort.

I Lived as their support, then we'll roam, knowing that our own dream was always home.

Defining Good Looks

When he speaks from the heart, it doesn't matter what he looks like, then you see his halo glisten because you don't look. You listen. Yet to truly see has always been our first mission. If he is brave and smart, humorous, charismatic, kind, witty, and benevolent with vision.....then Good looking? Well, he is the very definition.

What I'm After? After Friends

I imagine there is a line past satisfaction you pass when you finally win, that goes beyond the work, the where, the how and the when. I assume, from happiness, you never come back. Why do those enemies still attack? Who's to say they're not my friends when I win? Will winning confirm it? That even they would have to say that I deserve it?

One Sided

They said you were an accident, a chance,
And I gave my heart away with a glance.
But I know the Truth, that you were planned,
In a world where the hour glass always buries me with sand.

You always have that street smart,
that made me weep, it was so cool.
Thinking you'd Love me made me a fool!

I think we Love for security (like in a bet)
Yet, you were always so sure of me.
And I've missed the Love we lack (for two)
But follow your surety and always running back to you.

I Love Proof

I'm not crazy, and now, I Love proof. You crawled up into my mind, then treated me uncouth. You didn't Love me, so I was thinking and spinning, with the lies and suave moves. That is how you soothe, And you're the one who's winning. With a wish for you in my bed, yet always alone in my head, and like I said, "Now I need proof!"

So I'm not in Love with you. Test me and I'll act aloof! Like I said, I'm not in Love with you, and I'm not crazy too......Turns out, romantic wasn't True!

The lies you told, as Time goes by and you, grow old…The ones you'll fear were the ones to me so dear, the ones where you said, "I Love you" (and you said it like it was nothing too!)

As girls and Time go by, you'll hold your head so high.

Things may not be what you see, a test of faith, at that old birthday cake, Make a wish, there are plenty of fish, in the sea, if you like anyone (and on you'll move to what you'll be). One day I'll be the one and you'll prove that to me!

With gifts of little effort, those little words of Love and Truth, and in reality, my heart is relieved by that much needed proof.

Reality

My dreams still echo in my mind.
And in the face of reality, they are still all I want to find.
To build one in reality, I was too late
And to settle for reality, I took the bait.
But this I have!
Compared to reality, my dreams were great.

Alone

Alone is the world that left me in this lost and found.
Chained to this 'consideration as possible'. Helplessly bound.
Hope, yet alone, has got me under its spell.
Chasing a dream, cornered at the bottom of a well.
One moment in time… Oh yes! I was proud.
I scream your name from the gut, just soft. No! Just loud.

Though the passion I ignite for them, left my heart abating…
The humble, smarter, patient love lies waiting.

The Subway

Do you know how Lois Lane held onto Superman's hand when they were in the sky? If she let go she would die. Two hearts went for a fly.

That is how I grab onto your hand in the supermarket and at the gas station and in the subway!

The TV

They expected me to see all the blood.
And I was waiting for a man…
To put his hands over my eyes.

Then I saw the good-byes.
And I was waiting for a man…
To be stronger than me.

Then I was on my knees
And the TV was above me.
And I was still waiting for
Someone to love me.

Cheated

So, you cheated on me
And I drown in uncertainty.
I cheated on this test.
And then, I've cheated death.
Somedays I cheat myself
From a love poem I put up on my shelf.

So, who cheats us?
I could point the finger

But don't walk away.
Give me a little longer to linger.

From this great pool of life into which we delve…
Don't ask 'who cheats us?'
We cheat ourselves!

Faith is for ourselves and the miracle,
We make do with or without it.
So faith, there is something we can do about it.

Pretend

Where I hurt you I tell myself it's a farce
But how far does this joke go before it ends? A joke only a sage
could mend.
Was I just joking or is love pretend?

And some nights with you are too magical for us to part as
friends!
I'm in a dream and this love is pretend.

But the truth seems to come out when we lie,
And some nights there is so much truth my heart dies…
In the end…
Tell me my Love, will you pretend?

If I knew you too well, then where's the make believe?
With so much courage at first; all waiting to deceive.
And the whole point of it all is to see how far I'll bend…
If it's not you then it's make believe till the end and
If I profess too much, I guess it is time to pretend.

And all of Life is just a waste unless
It is on my whole Love that it is based unless,
It makes a truth of this mission I've faced.
Will Truth take us some place that we can't see?
Stop…soften…hurry…flee!
And come pretend with me.

Superman

I am falling from this chopper.
This machine of immortal ingenuity.
-     It failed
-     It failed, the fake thing,
And now I am lowered and caught,
And now spitting out these goofy words
And everything I sought, into
My shaky palm, lowered and
Caught
On your rising chest
And on each precious thought.

My words aren't always goofy,
And my hand doesn't always shake,
Yet I don't catch *them* when *they* land
And I know now Planes are fake
And here it falls to earth and
You've caught it anyway, although you
Aren't from earth at all.
You see I never saw me fall, But
If I too could fly, would I? Well, I guess that's why you
Catch us and I guess that's why girls
Sigh,
Anyway, this all must bore you, so
I'll make it short and sweet, so now please be
Gentle as you put me on my feet and before you fly off
And before you make a leap.

Don't tell me all you know then
It scares me half to death.
And before I go away now to marry
Bob or Seth. I'll say
Each shaky word's for you then.

I saw it land there on your chest,
It's not much for sure I know,
To not feel what mortals feel;
Must understand a superhero's mind,
A heart more mortal,
With
A chest of steel.

And I'm no superhero, so I can't penetrate
Through steel, but
They will fly around you too, those
Birds with sinking hearts,
A superhero's woo, and
One brave one will fly faster than you,
And then what will you do?
Will you go crazy?
I *know* now, that's the price,
Filling hearts what's made you nice,
And the rest can be enticed. So,

Come with me and we'll walk the streets,
Not fly,
And sometimes we'll even cry, and wonder what its like
To fly, and I hope that you don't die.

But anyway, that's only mortal, and
You've got a job to do, so, you
Can count on the girls you've caught and
Penetrate through their chests too, as I lay here
Counting sheep, but,
Not waiting for you, No!

So what should I say to Bob and Seth?
How do I ask *them* not to go?

But in the end, I know I win!
They will soon disintegrate in my mind
And like the feather you caught,
Will soon fly.

Up, up, and away!

But I hope that someday, you will
Swoop down on me and take, these
Mortal thoughts into your cape and
Like the hate that will
Disintegrate into the air and

FLY
Up, up, and away.
Up, up, and away.

You Hurt Me

I say your name weakly, as my weakness.
Your absence governs my cigarettes and my cleanliness.
I like to sulk that my hardship has no witness.
But comfort that my pen can give tribute to my tenderness
And to your distraction and indifference.

Reverend Night

We met night like he was our church.
Our bed was a sinner, and all the stars, our confessionals.
The cross made our characters.
The talk was our hymnals, and
Our laughter, it had to be God.

So, our laughter was our proof of Reverend Night in the wee hours of
morning.

Restless

A cloud sits restless in my head,
And all the morals of your bed,
Is the proximity of your skin.

And you wonder where my mind has been!

Women's Lib.

You don't open the door and you don't get the check!
There is a line between what is chivalrous and what is respect.
Or kind!
So, don't treat me like a man just because I have a mind.

A Different Style, A Different Girl

I guess you can call me too serious.
Style over substance makes me furious.
Believe me, I won't want to be you just because my arms get flappy.
And although we don't see eye to eye,
I need to protect you if you're happy.
Yet, I wish you wanted more than to have all the boys crave you!
So, Good luck in your Life
And I hope that fashion can save you.

Weakness

Pride has a way of making people look weaker than they are.
And the weakness when you are in Love requires a bow from the
human spirit afar.
When you are in Love, only one is Good enough,
And weakness makes it worse when you are tough!
So, I guess a defensive man acts like a little boy and True Love
makes a man act just a little coy.
As you always push my brain to the brink
And so defenseless because my will is weak.

Delusion?

When I am down, God is there in my future, present and past too. When
I can't face something, sometimes I am saved in the nick of Time, so I
turn it into rhyme... something you didn't see (but nothing gets past you)!
God can be scary, enlightening, and kind, if I am in a bind (then I believe
the last two.) And I believe God does exist because He has to! Maybe I
imagine Someone superior to my mind, Who thinks above, an imaginary
Friend who teaches me to Love, and to feel until He is real!

The Truth of What You Make

From inside you, into the world, only one thing comes out........the
Truth. So, make it Good!

Punishment for the Bad

When you punish a person, you shouldn't punish the Good part of that
person.

Your Work Left Up To Luck?

You put your heart and soul into your work, and then, leave it all up to chance, with its spells and curses? Basing the success of your work on luck undermines its purpose. But although it is your mission, and the chance could always lurk, you are more of a miracle than your work.

Possibility Starts In Your Mind

I can do something amazing with my obsession, if I stay focused and away from digression. Armed with only my thoughts and contained passion (feels like I'll burst) and always, always, always think first. Now I flaunt my ability when they were blind to my possibility, that I could slam dunk it........ who'd have thunk it?

Changes Of The Fairy Tale Thoughts

My heart was sure of you, determined and serene. I spent my Life chasing a dream. You are too Good for me, so other people pointed at me and said, "What a waste!". You are my nourishment, but I Live with just a taste. I say then, "Like he did to my Fate, he disrupts and he rearranges". But this dream doesn't really die. It changes, from a fairy tale thought to knowing I'll never be your wife, to a goal that keeps my heart growing, which is to get on with my Life.

An Illusion Of Good

Without him, he still makes you blue. He has that irrational power over you. Those memories that you can recall (nothing) but that he can enthrall. Bottom line is, he is too Good to be True, is a way of saying that nobody can have it all.

Staying Young

Youth makes us bolder, and you look to me for answers, since I am older. You desperately want my regard, desperate for the freedom from the Time being young you served., You know you've worked hard and got the happiness you deserved, happy that what is done is done, growing up to what you've begun, And I know in the long run, that keeps you young. But what you don't know is distain, from strife that makes a heart leary. What you don't know is dismay! Let's see if we can keep it that way!!

A Life Proving A Broken Heart

That boy broke my heart when I was delirious. When he said he Loved me, I thought he was serious. Turns out he was teasin', in a world where Love was the word, but temperaments change like a season. I thought I held the upper hand from the start, but it was his. They told me, "There is no rhyme or reason", to him breaking my heart. But my Life says, "There is!".

Good All The Way

With being bad, I recognize it, because I know cynicism, skepticism and doubt. But I am so Good (with my witticisms), I wear myself out, Until I am all the way Good, just about!

Mind Control

The effort to think without you...... must there be the pain? Bottom line is, I trusted your brain. You are braver than me. You've gone farther than me, and you are smarter than me, is something an inner voice told me. It knows you. So I don't mind if you control me since I chose you.

Getting Above the Tops

I am always intrigued by those mysterious things you hid. I am scared when you are stern. I Love you for everything you did. And I Love you even if I get nothing in return. I say you can't top yourself with Truth because you can't get above what's True. But in reality, there's no way you can ever top my Love for you!

The Definition

If what they say is shallow in you can be made to be skin deep, let me fill in the spaces. Your character leaves them all behind. All that's left is the traces. Besides, maybe we wear out our character on our faces! In your smile, clues of who you are left a hint. But appearances are temporary (Love is permanent). If you are kind, intelligent, charismatic, humorous, quick, honest and brave, you are a treasure to save. And if to Love you makes a mission, then Good looking? Well, you are the very definition.

Seeing the Future

We see identity within our hearts, but when you look at me, I realize I'm only a peasant.
The knowledge and mystery of the past is in your eyes, looking like the moon (a crescent).
And your face is always the future to me, at present.

A Prayer After We're Fine

I think you and I could help each other if we could call each other "mine". But what if we were fine? This world left us separate and made me desperate and turned my prayer into a whine, a secret that was once Love. But once we're fine, who then do I think of? I understand the faithless, but not the tasteless. So I've savored and I've craved, praying for so long, conceiving things with my brain (I've flexed), one thing after the next,

31

and proud that I've behaved. But what will be my prayer after, finally, I am saved?

Sometimes What Alone Means

I face the world single handedly, while you are doubley on my mind. Whenever you speak, you speak first candidly. Nothing can leave you and I behind! We are on our own and isolation is the storm we must weather. I must be alone, knowing you are alone. So we're alone together.

Believe

Sometimes, in this world, suffering has gone way past my crying. Everything will be O.K. is what I'm selling, but you're not buying. I tell you, "Everything will be O.K.", and my mind gets away with it. You call me an actress. It's easier to say than to stay with it in practice. The proof isn't in what I said because we're apart, when what I think is in my head and what I know is in my heart. I say, "Everything will be O.K.", and you are buying it, even though I know nothing. But everything will be O.K. so we are trying it, And that's got to count for something!!

"Ignorance Is Bliss"

The defense against evil is; I don't understand.

Aging For Love

Once upon a Time turned out to be less than once in a while. But when I was young, romantic wasn't my style. I see what's inside you when you frown or smile, even just a little bit, which seems to be harder the older we get. At a young age, we're so bold, and then comes doubt. But I think growing old turns us inside out. Proof is; to the faithless, the lesson you've learned and you've told, without clout. That is; what Loving them is all about, as God sets the stage. I mean, you Love you even as you age!

The Full Life Belief

People will say that you have it all, but only in their affirmation do you stand tall. And only in a glass that's full can you call a glass half-full. And while you are scrambling around for those other halves, you are missing out on what I have! With your greed to win all things, you forget to Love the small things. And your Life is full after all you underwent with your elite (I suppose we can meet in the middle), and with your wonderment, you ask me, "How can you be happy with so little?", You can't understand why we're happy but we are. You see, once you have it all, you forget to wish upon a star.

At Death's Door

My Life denies my death's woe, each without you. When I die, I don't go. I go through.

You Haven't Got A Prayer

If you haven't said a prayer yet, maybe that's why you haven't had one.

Front Line Workers

Even before they help, they know they could die, and by their actions, they hold their heads up high. In society, for courage and bravery, we've set the bars. They risk their Lives to rescue ours. And with these bars, we understand each other. They say, "I'll show you!". But with this cowardice I have, it's hard to know you. The heart is a muscle they've flexed, And they will be rewarded in this Life or the Next. Everyone's goal is to be a part of something that lasts, and everything else is like a con. This I know; Acts of kindness go on and on and on and on.

Happier

Romance makes us sappier from a hungry Love that we have tasted. If you don't want to make someone happier, Love has been wasted.

Seeing My Imagination

Who you actually are has to be unveiled, but I failed, because I only saw what I wanted to believe. You see, someone sees differently when their heart is on their sleeve. Even if I'm not a saint, I stand by you with a heart that is faint, and real Love for me is still long overdue. But just because I see with a heart that's True, doesn't mean you do!

The Entrance for the Faithless

When I spend my Life dreaming away, this fear inside me makes me pause. And it is never just seeming that way when I stood for a cause. And then, I must have invited all the faithless into my world to disrupt. But if I go down, I go down standing up.
And I am different than them, I pray. Yet they say, "It is always the same us"! So if I enter a room when I'm famous, I don't want them to stand, stay seated says my head....... I want the hair on the backs of their necks to stand up.

Don't Ask, Don't Tell

Don't ask if you are right or wrong, and your dreams, don't ask if they must take so long! Don't ask if you are weak or strong, knowing strength comes from up above....... Ask if you can Love!
Don't ask if you have poverty or wealth, when you ask for how long you'll have Good health, or those confessions, made apparent or in stealth (you know they are what you're thinking of!) Ask if you can Love! Don't ask for men or for what your weakness or insecurity brings, don't ask if with those narrow minded lies, he stings! Don't ask for all these petty things (when it comes to push and shove)....... Just ask if you can Love!

One Love With Courage

If you liked me, that would change me. Instead you stole my heart and you rearrange me. You told me that, the way I like you, it will never last, And then your dark shadow was cast, in my mind, is where you lurk. Well, I have other reasons to like you besides making it work. So I keep my distance, but fall in Love whenever the mood does strike me. You see, I Love you even when you don't like me!

Who Would Approve of Suffering?

After unrequited Love (like the myth too!) pain was all you could prove. If you suffer, I know God is with you, but He probably doesn't approve.

How Far You'll Go... Does He Meet You Half Way?

The Love you had for him started in your head, where they said, "She creates It", in a world where Beauty Lives, where imagination has the vision that Gives. They say, "You made a mistake Loving him and you are the only one that doesn't hate it". Your sacrifice over him was too severe (But everything seemed so clear!) So now you Love him and nothing abates It. Yeah, you went crazy for him. The question is; Does he appreciate it??

Second First Impression

You didn't like me from the beginning even though I was always grinning and I learned my lesson, that there is no second chance for a first impression.

Life

It is not to defeat death, or to look forward to death, or to even give death consideration! It is to find something more important than death.

Worldly

Since we don't have a history, and what is new to me remains a mystery, I'll give you the benefit of the doubt, and since you mean the world to me and I Live without, on what is True, I'll take your word. When I am alone with you, I'm alone with the world.

Having A Future

The past was my future at one point and of some sort. And since it got me here, it was a comfort. But I've been late.
And whenever my mind doesn't roam, the present is my home, at any rate. For those memories I need, as of yet, I'll find them with you (is a Good bet).
But the toughest question I ask myself is, "When does the future get great?".

What Goes First, What Goes Last

In Life, sometimes, I have no control in the end, but I had a friend! When God strips us of everything (and losing laughter would be the worst). But I do have control over what goes first, from my Fate! I hope it's the hate!! I've learned to have a friend to teach me what I know. If God strips us of our knowledge, from long ago, I have control over what is the last to go (because they are all I'm thinking of). It's Faith and Love!

Crazy Inside

For every move we make, there is a history. And in the long run, each person is a mystery. When I am with you, involuntarily, I am confiding, to your story of Love where neither one of us is hiding. A story anyone of us can sink our teeth into. And unafraid of the Life I've made, you meet me and say, "Don't worry! I know what is underneath you".

Reasoning

When you are thinking about doing something bad, you're not thinking.

Trusting People

You've said, "Some dreams are possible and some are impossible". If it is only possible in someone's head, you said, "They are far away!". But who's to say?
These dreams, the more impossible they are, is maybe because of how impossible you set the bar! So, far away and in multitude, lies a star. Before Goodness was here, Goodness was conceived. And sometimes, people are misunderstood before they are perceived (and redeemed). But trust in them? I will, once I am believed, for my dream.

Asking For More

You were known for your Good looks and your charm. Not for your veracity. Yet my heart called out to you as, "Your Majesty", when you noticed me, like in a romance of Ladies and Lords. Sometimes, when we Love, all that's real is the words. For you to Love me (how you enthrall!) and for that to be True, was all I asked for, if I can recall. I guess no one can have it all!

Difference Makes People Interesting

'What you do to the least of us, you do to me' said a King from up above. If I fear everyone who is odd, who balance me and I shy away from the way they challenge me, my mind is closed to a new way they are thinking of. Being scared of the different can harm your ability to Love.

Hope Has Control

They Loved you when you were young (not meek), for being confident by tongue and cheek, and Living Life so full. But they laughed at your crush, and thought it trivial. They say, "Some have encountered more heartache than this, so get over him instead!". But that is not what all your Hope said.

Denied The Perfect Man

To survive this world, we Live however we can and our inner strength comes through. Like secrets, we confide them. You say, "I'm doing well without a man," but that's because I was denied them.

We Can't Overestimate Love

I can find meaning in your communication, but there, you don't state me. You like to run from Love, but you underestimate me. I walk toward you like I own the world, which I give to you in the motion. But then you laugh at me for being a silly girl with a fairy tale notion. It's a high bar, I know, but a prince is what my Fate is made of. After the work I've done in the dirt to rise above. You laugh, but you're wrong. You can't overestimate Love.

Faking Brave??

Talking to you, I realize, _f I was brave, I could fake pretty, charming and smart. It is believing in myself, is a Good start. Like that memory of talking to you (was all I save). Because you can fake almost anything. But you can't fake brave!

Overlooking a Broken Heart

My heart breaks again without emotion. Just the end of a fool's notion. My mind is set on a romance I had, caught up in captions. A dream within a price, the heartache, but not just sad. Just something that happens.

Thinking Of You Is Me

I'll stop thinking of myself first, and think of you until my heart feels it will burst, so that you'll respect me and Love me... But aren't I still thinking of me?

Is Love Invisible?

This deep Love of mine, at your feet, and so discreet. A Love not meant to tease, made into a prayer from on my knees. I don't even say, "Please, Love me! Let me lead for you to follow me!". I just say, "Acknowledge me!".

What Are They Hiding?

Evil is obvious when it hides, because it hides. What does Good have to hide??

My Joke

Honey, I told a joke the other day, with that spirit. It was funny, so you pray. That joke, you said to everyone listening to behold it, and you are so proud of me, you thought you told it. Then our heads filled with the joy of their laughter. And that was all the proof we needed for our happily ever after!

Knowing Your Side

If you are on the wrong side and you win, you won't know it because, to get there, you sin. And if the wrong side is what you're choosing, eventually you'll know it because you'll never stop losing. I bet victory means you don't hide anything, and without effort, the Truth, you show It. If you are on the right side, you'll know it!

You Can Be Rich

Somedays I love my Fate, better than some memories, by far! The more you appreciate, the richer you are. This dream that took me to a star, well, you've been it, when I appreciate Life down to every minute. My heart hopes true wealth will come forth and lets me know what a penny is worth. As long as I'm alive, my dream is real. We are rich or poor based on how we feel.

Whose Consequence?

He stole your heart like theft and you've been looking for it ever since. Unfortunately you remember how he broke your heart over and over until nothing made sense. But worst of all, he ignored you and took away your confidence. So did you overestimate yourself, and now you're Living with the consequences of Loving too much on a whim? Or maybe you just overestimated him!!

No Pride

I've had a dream for decades, and you've been it, that keeps my head in the clouds and my feet off the ground. It hurts you so, about this dream, that my heart is in it, because it breaks your heart to turn me down. But between this bittersweet battle with men, to Love, I will try again and push a few things aside (the rest with nothing left to hide!) and you'll say, "Wow! That girl has no pride".

Love Isn't Easy

It is so hard to get a chance to Love someone who is easy to Love!

Art

The best art tells us things we already know.

A Prayer To Remember You

This Life pushed and shoved you. When you die inside, I know for sure how much I Love you. I talk to that knowledge instead of you. And it hurts that I put nothing ahead of you. To that knowledge, I never lie. I will wait for a reply, no matter how popular or odd. I believe there is a God!

What You Think Of Me

Your character so excels, that when I'm with you, I'm hearing bells. You can say, "My minion Loves me!". So Heaven is as high as your high opinion of me.

The Conversation

When I defend myself, it is survival of the fittest (in a way). So when I bear my heart and soul to you, you have nothing to say and monopolize the conversation. To hear me, you ignore first and beseech less. Either way, I left you speechless!

The Rescue

With you, I guess I don't Love. I savor. And if I could alleviate your pain, you'd be doing me a favor. I Love the future and the past, but mostly, the present. Putting your mind at ease is a present. Because, for once in the world, I've found you and you were no compromise. So when I rescue you, it's like I won a prize. Finally I stop thinking of how I behave and pay attention to my mission: It is you I save!

Jesus; The Evil That Was Beneath You

You prayed with fear for your Life (which you could restore), but you hated evil more! Your Life was for us and the beggars and the thieves. Your wounds were meant to heal me, yet they say, "For His suffering, she grieves". But your Life? There was so much more to it! And the evil that you hated? Even when you suffered, you refused to resort to it. We Love the least of us, then for Him, look toward a timeline and a steeple. Since He was a king disguised as one of the people.

Being Poor

When you are doing without, and making do, it is like you have conquered deficiency. So, in a way, you are doing with!

Listen To Your Heart

They point their finger at me and say, "With men, you accept whatever comes your way!". But is that what the pot calls the kettle? And you like him. When that stops, their next question is, "How far will you settle?". If you lose Love, one day you'll find it is your soul you peddle, in a world where evil's main goal in Life is to meddle.

Thinking

Passion is thinking. And any thinking of bad or evil (to do) isn't even thinking.

Life Is Hard

You weren't honest with me, but you played your card and left me on the brink. Life all around is hard is not what I wish, but what I think. Each of us, in our own way, turns the page, may be punished by Fate, in a cage. So there is no reason to hate as we age.

The Beggar

I started my Time on you greedy for Love from whom I adore. I wanted more, more, more. Now I piddle. My overabundance of feeling for you met your indifference to me. But I don't give up when there is still the middle. So, I told God I'd compromise if you could just Love me a little.

Summed Up In A Word

All my memories that have helped and all the Love I've felt or missed, everytime I never raised my fist, plus the protection from my nightmares (since some disrupt)………God sums it up.

The Possibility Of Your Dream

If I Love a ton, I chase my dream simply because it's fun. And each little step proves (to me), it can be done.

Trying

Always desiring the best of what I want.....Do I get any better? My lack of character means we won't ever be together. But I can't deny that Cupid's Love did strike me in a world where you could never like me. That I know, which pushes my character below. Sometimes you have to have faith in what is behind you or above you. And I do! God never lied. I've said, "I Love you". Well, I tried.

Evaluating After Him

He couldn't steal my Life even though he tore my heart in halves. The more you appreciate what you've truly got, the more you have. Life with him is a Life how he can always decree It. But maybe Life without him isn't sad, but how I see it!

Time To Not Worry

In this Life we have to stand on our own, with only a wish from people to stay strong. When things in this world get easy, I think, there must be something wrong. Since in reality,he and I don't belong. Yet in my mind, we were a perfect match. Is there a day I don't have to worry without any strings attached? Where my heart is light and breezy? Where I don't have to say, "Nothing in this Life is easy!"?

Are You With Him For Love or Pleasure

Over the years, pleasure, where does it go?
Over the years, Love, where does it not go?

Love

I had to be in control before I could surrender to someone.

Fate's Fabrication

I believe some bad luck is deliberate.

People Change

I understand that people are punished. I just don't understand why they were punished permanently!

Having Nothing

Once I realized I had nothing, I could realize my dream (that was all or nothing). That is how you made it seem! And it is always what I choose. Because I had nothing, I had nothing to lose. So I ask you to meet me somewhere in the middle. Because this dream of mine is so big and I'd settle for so little.

The Fall And The Spin

Everytime I meet you, I learn (my nervous glare becomes so stern). Will my Love for you mean my catastrophic fall or will I win all in all? I spin and I fall seeing you, the weight of my mind is lifted, like an earthquake, the floor has shifted, by the concern in your smile. My mind then spins so I turn and turn a little while. We dance and I spin, looking for something I wouldn't give for a grin. This dance is where I talk to you, looking for a secret password, and forge ahead, knowing I can't go backward, to a smile in a dream so exciting….. We face reality, whether restrictive or inviting.

What Is Reason In Love?

You can't depend on the foolish, but he stays with you because he adores you (if you don't abuse it!). To save your Life, reason is always there for you. So use it! In Love, you were awkward and he was so seasoned. Sometimes the reason in Love is to be happy for no reason.

The Hermit

They say, "Why are you a hermit?". But they can't know my Life unless they've been through It! You either find yourself in a corner because you chose it* or you were backed into it. God said, "You want what you want, but here is your Fate. I've insisted". And yes! I did choose my corner, but, honestly, my arm was twisted!

*"Inside Man" movie

Cupid's Aim

You have a perfect Love with another and then you say I could have that with someone else someday, that spark between us like a flame. But really, if it is not you I'm with, could Love ever be the same? Aside from Cupid, there is no one left to blame.

Measuring My Time

I finally know where I'm at by your eyes and God's grace. And you have the judgment of my Life by the look on your face. Sometimes I can pass by but sometimes I'm out of place. When I stand in front of you today, it could go either way. I could kiss you. With our conversation, I dance around the issue like a pantomime. I Love you like them and you say, "That and a dime!" But I still know the calm that comes from being at the right place at the right Time!

Getting Old

At one point in Time, the passion behind your eyes was what you told,
And because I couldn't match your wit, I bit my tongue. God made your
face to get old, But because I'm never tired of it, you will always be young.

Sin and Guilt

Better not to punish yourself!! That is Someone Else's job.

Angels

Have you ever heard of angels trying to save someone who
did not want to be saved?
I've worked and I've slaved!
Give me what is my due…
Angels, I tired of listening to you.

These humans down here on earth won't have it done because
they can't do it themselves.
And down here on earth the heart, it swells, it delves…
Where it pleases
These angels, they are teases.
Give me what is my due!
Angels, I'm tired of seeing you.

You see, they are saving someone who in a round-about way
has always been chaste.
And what is the point of this life that we've faced?
Angels, give me my due,
I'm so tired of mimicking you.

Angels, you said it was to be my first, I said…
It was to be the last,
With so many firsts you see…

So out of them, who is left to end this curse?
Angels, give me my due,
So, I can start believing in you.

Never Ending Chances

1st chance….. I have the spirit to flaunt. They must see the passion for what I want!
2nd chance….. I don't give up, that's what I'm knowing. And they'll see me again because I keep going.
3rd chance….. Didn't they see how I've desired? They must be crazy to not choose me and I'm so tired.
4th chance….. I Love myself in each chance, and I've cared. Maybe those other Times, I was unprepared.
It is not winning, but our efforts that prove who we are, especially by these chances, how we've come this far. Maybe in reality, I'm not a star, but the test is my Life that no one can mar. So it's that Life, that over and over, where my enemies pry, to find
I'm a beggar for one more try.

Marilyn

When real life beats the theater,
Independence, freedom of a dove.
My life is the stuff movies are made of.
I came from an orphanage and the sky was going to be blue.
I made beauty true.
True as it seems
And I made sex an impossible dream, and
They can't say I was unsociable,
Because it was real but untouchable,
And I hardly will ever show it,
I made it hard for poets,
To make anything good enough for me, anything that wasn't lame
Since 'magic' was my middle name!

Pretty

Marilyn wore her heart on her sleeve and
Her soul on her face!

Shakespeare Relived

I've lived long , going to the 'house of song', the masquerade ball, not
knowing who was right and wrong.
He caught my eye,
But one look always says "Good-bye"...
First.

Do we have to be Romeo and Juliet?
If you don't show up in my life,
Will you show up at my death?
And watch me leap from a grave that is so boring
That can't keep me from exploring,
Your eyes and hearing your lips, apart,

You remember when I tripped going up the stairs to meet you?
Remember, you stood on a pedestal. But then I tripped. And then I was
on the pedestal, but your memory slipped. And where I stood to sense
the past... I gave it up to fate at last!

You said, "It is better to be safe than sorry" with a look that said, "Slows
down" and "Calm down". But Juliet can't. It's not in her. Our Romeo
and Juliet is a puppet show. Fate pulls the strings until we have a tangled
end.

And I couldn't say that I would be gone loud enough for you to hear me.
But of course maybe you did... Shakespeare relived!

Thinking The Same

No matter how hard I try, I can't get Fate to work for me. Since, in Love, I lose (but I don't lose sorely). Singly, am I punished for sinning with men? What is a Life without Love? And Fate is winning again! Friends and enemies go on without a name, but I suppose my punishment is tame, compared to then, after I Loved a boy, (where Fate and I were thinking the same). Because I slowly learn how to think on my own (and in my deepest thoughts of you, I've never been alone!). So, Fate, or you, decided that Love would strike me. But I won't waste my Time on anyone so crazy they don't like me! Yet when anyone interrupts my Life, for Good or bad, I am forced to pay attention, And Loves Live past punishment and thrive past redemption

Going For Guts

Having to prove your courage will find you. You don't have to go looking for it.

The Miracle That Makes Everything Matter

What doesn't matter after you know you are alive?

Graduating Thought

Once you know you are going to be O.K., and you stop being scared for yourself, your happiness begins to depend on somebody else. So when we think of our independence (that we made), you make me think of you as aid, and give up our crutch for joy for someone else. It helps.

The Focus on Happy

God makes most people happy at least once before they die. It's our choice to choose which to focus on!

The Brave Romantic

What makes a romantic so brave? How does he know what to say or how to behave? When he approaches me there'll be courage written all over his face, and that only something to trace, regrets from his past, will give him humility and Grace.

I write now past all the rejection I survived, and therefore all the Love that's been deprived. I can move on because of the little bit of fearlessness I save, and I ask, "What makes a romantic so brave?"

Being Popular

Not everybody likes me and I feel the need to please, so I change. I change until I'm perfect. But then, nobody likes me!

True Love

I wanted to be religious, but those sacred vows! I just don't understand (like for other vows I can). My religion has been to worship what is tempting in man. There is my own penance (with so many men). You see my heart gets trampled on again and again. With my attraction and when I can't think straight, I need a blessing of thoughts on whom I should be thinking of. But I've never been wise. There is a compromise from above, And that is, I want to Love who God wants me to Love.

Restricted To Reason

He said, when he insulted me, it was underrated. But it wasn't (since the insult was stated)! Later, he says, "Oh, I'm just teasin'!" What is funny is, like most insults, it was made for no reason. If you are just being rude, that can still impair. But I examined my heart and found something that is unfair. And that is, insults are sly. They come at you unexpectedly, while you are dishing the dirt. But if there is truly no reason for his insult, why would it hurt?

There Is A Meaning

If Life were meant to be frivolous, why would It be so difficult? There was punishment for pleasure after those men. I looked in their eyes. Love and loss. You were the cost and the one I prized. If there were no point to Life, why do we get chastised? And why would Its meanings always catch me by surprise?

Mothers

Mother,

I feel a responsibility when I see your pride in me. And because of you, I may be aware of what a free ride can be, since I am the world to you whenever the world gets colder, and you carry those worlds on your shoulder. You are the treadmill that moves my steps to where I'm going and the first one to teach me what I'm knowing. You've done everything first as we stand in line and say, "Better you then me". So with or without you, someday I'll look up to what a dream (so True) can be.

Crazy Enough To Ask

You make me crazy in my heart and in my mind? Disrupting too! Yet you're better than the rest and I raise my cup to you. And I ask Someone for the courage to Live up to you. Until I find my peace in art (poems and lyricals)….. Sometimes I ask for miracles.

The Worst I Believe

Shall I conceive that you'll surprise me with something like love up your sleeve? That Fate makes Life for us together since there is nothing lost not possible to retrieve? Shall I desire the stars in your eyes like the ones in the skies that never leave to stay? That I will never Love then leave men. Why not? There are worse things to believe in!

Considering A Dream

You were a dream before I saw you as my dream. You are beautiful and smart, courageous with a heart, And those possibilities of you and I only start… in my head, where you say, "You Love me but I Love you instead!" But I know you're a kidder too, as well as kind. My dream is that we're possible, but only in my mind, where I consider you.

Winning

In order to beat me, they have to be able to Live as me.

Rags To Riches

Sometimes it takes realizing you have nothing to realize you need everything.

Sometimes Fair

If something is given to you unfairly, it is something you can never have. I believe you Loved me barely, and left me somewhere between happy and sad. Maybe you are that something that I never had! Like a glass half full, there are Times you care, and I put those in rhymes. So, yes! Life is fair (at Times).

In Your Hands

I stay at home and don't work at my dream. Meanwhile, I lose my confidence and my self esteem. Basically, I get bored! You have to do things yourself to really receive a reward (So it must mean something, and what you have to lose is nothing!) I'm honest to myself as I'm confessing, that I must work on me since it is my hands held out for a blessing! And I say to the cynic who bores, "My dreams are in my hands, not yours!"

Facing Life With Love

Love elevates us to another dimension. Given a chance "I Love you" wasn't something (I forgot to mention.) And you did, but word gets around. My dream man swept me off my feet until they couldn't reach the ground. For a while in this world, there wasn't evil, ugliness or strife. But then you realize, just because you're in Love, doesn't mean you don't have to face Life.

Proof

In this thing we call 'Life', we need the Truth. And with all the strife we survive, we show God proof. With the burden on my shoulders, I feel so mired down beyond my crying. So the proof is; Why am I so tired if I'm not trying?

Whoever

You like whoever you can and make fun of me for choosing to Love a dream man. But you're not alone (which was your plan), like me. And the rest of men.....the rest, why should you even care? You see, my dream man is the best of them..... And the best, why shouldn't I like him (with my heart so bare) when you like whoever's there??

Value Over Fear

I don't work hard because my Time is limited. I work hard because my Time is valuable.

Decision

He said he Loved me but he was a bluffer. And that's when I learned, you have faith or you suffer. I can prove myself over and over again but I'm no one they carry. My Time is full but I tarry. And over the mountain I climb is where denial will lurk. I have faith or I work.

My Job

I think, in Life, you have to have aim. And my job on earth lies in my brain. When someone asks me, "Who are you, "Ma'am?", my job is to think for myself until I know who I am. As I Live, opinions change, bravery goes up then down, and passions swell and wane, always knowing my other job..... trying to stay sane.

Hero Worship

I've built you up inside my mind. When Fate breaks us down, you remain kind. The benevolence of your deeds and Good judgment (where it leads) make me feel like your heart is on your sleeve. You are my ideal, I believe. With our little blessings how can we say we have zero? This is what it's like to worship a hero.

The Reverie Sun

I Love he and she, us and we, her and them. I Loved him, until he made me blue. I Love you! I know because it is you I'm thinking of. The broken heart he gave me though, made me forget True Love and everything under a reverie sun. Isn't it easier to just Love everyone?

Loving By Will Standing

Love sometimes is all or nothing, and I stand by It to stand for something. It comforts me when I'm alone and makes nothing unclear, because you were still not there. So I stand by Love against all odds, with a heart, not mine but God's. Still I stand by Love by sheer force of will, and when I do, Time stands still.

The Warning To My Heart

I wished on a star above you! Should I Love you? Like on a whim. I Love everyone and you are one of them. But it is you I think of. Are you the 'One and Only' I truly Love? Then who identified? True Love is Love intensified. Especially if you're a stranger. But I should know going after True Love creates more danger.

Chess

"All is fair in Love and war" as long as I care before I blink. I vow to hurt no one in this lore........ A fairy tale that's fair, I think. My dream is to lay my head down upon your chest, and forget, those conversations where I'm at war and wind up playing chess.

Surrender To Faith

You're a brainiac and you won't take a leap of faith?? Why are we too afraid of being wrong, thinking about faith instead of having it?

Joy Or Justice

I would have felt Love for you, with a kiss, is how I seal It. When I do know Love for you, I Live It. You have to feel joy before you can give it. I chased you with my heart (forward and backward is where I start). And I never lied. Not men, but the perfect man, is what I've been denied. From backed into a corner, I tried. Now when I think of you, it hurts, and I say, "Must it?". And if you ever think of me, maybe I didn't bring joy, but I brought Justice!

Who Has The Power?

Most of your enemies only have something if you're thinking of them.

Running

When I'm all Loving, I look you in the eyes. When I sin, the only place I'm looking is over my shoulder.

The Window In The Room

You're enticing me with Life by a window pane. I see you with excitement, but in my past remains the pain. You attract me like light from my window in a cold, lonely room. I make up these memories and that is where you loom. The light could even mean a way to heaven (and that is where you left your mark). But how do I ever really get out of this room when I'm always in the dark?

Partly Good

So you used to be a bad girl (no doubt). But people have marveled at how much you've changed. The hate you used to feel has fizzled out and the lion inside you is tame. But the Love from before you were born is there when you smile or pout. God probably marvels at how much you've stayed the same!

The Blessing

Sometimes it is probably not your fault that a blessing doesn't come your way. But it is always your fault when you don't appreciate it!

People

The singer helps me to sing the last stanza,
When I start to lose time,
When I'm out of tune and sing the blues.

The dancer tugged at my soul,
When I became overweight,
When I lacked rhythm,
When I needed to see someone else.

The actor leads me to the end of the movie,
When I don't know which way to turn,
When I can act no more.

The poet reminds me to love,
When I see myself,
When there is nothing left for them to remind me of.

The man takes her to his castle,
When she forgets she is a woman.
Like a mother who reminds her child that life can be, well,
Wonderful!

And all together,
Ah!...INVINCIBLE.

The Blessing

There is touch and sight, taste and smell and sound too.
If you assess correctly, there are blessings all around you!

Evil is on the Inside

If inner beauty was judged like outer beauty, we would love each other
every little bit!
And some people are still trying to see how ugly they can get.

Thinking only of Yourself

If you are self centered, eventually something will be wrong with you. So
what do you focus on then?

Honest Accusation

You want to pretend I'm not a Good person, so you attack my character,
something I hold sacred. Your motive isn't pretend. It's hatred. I know
I am a Good person. Your existence spreads doubt. But it's your lie and
you're selling it, with me or without. A lie tells more about the person
who's telling it then the person it's about.

Men and Money

My attempts to make money have been feeble. Money can be dispensed sparsely, scarcely, or in a mad sum. Money is the root of all evil. But still! I wish I had some!
When I fell in Love, it was like looking in a mirror and all I saw was double. When he broke my heart, people said, "He treated her bad, Son!" So now, all guys can bring me is trouble….. But I still wish I had one!

Only Way To Say Good-bye

When we add our Lives up, we analyze the sums. But when the Time comes for us to say, "Adieu", I remember saying, "Hi", to you. I fly to you. I fly. There are so many ways to say, "Good-bye".
Maybe I was like those other girls….. really worlds away, but not so different. I think, when you said, "Good-bye", you were indifferent. Or there was no more Love to send, and you were glad to see things end. Two people hating each other, and too tired to face that danger. Maybe we said, "Good-bye" out of anger. But that doesn't erase what lasts above, or our past Love, old and new. I think my Love was True. So before I say "Good-bye" to an unrequited Love so high, I can already say I miss you, by my need. The only way you should say "Good-bye" is to plead, that God be with you!

On: 'Splendor in the Grass' You're The Treasure

Christ's warning is: "Lay not up treasures for yourself on earth. Lay up for yourself treasures in heaven…For where your treasure is, there will your heart be also"
   I get from this that I have a treasure where is my worth.
Oh! This I know;
You are not on earth!

Test Of The Detached

It is in a different way I grieve, watching others with sad phrases, and how we coin them.
For someone, it is my heart I finally retrieve, or I will join them.

The Dream Deserved

If your dream shares Love with the world, you got what you deserved, who their Love was directed at.
But if your dream of Love was meant for you alone, you deserve much more than that!

Good is God and God is Good

Maybe in this ocean of humanity, mutually speaking, we're not all separable. But when people come together for bad, it's irreparable. So I will go down with this ship, reputably, if it is worthy and sensible. And when people come together for Good, we're nothing but invincible.

The Fairness To Be Shielded

We represent the world to you and yet, you tell all to befriend us. But when the news and gossip get so gory or horrendous, you have to know. Is it fair that so do we? So I say, "Shield me!". When we tell history with disgusting tales, do we spare the innocents all the messy details? Someone goes from laborious to notorious and with a crime, there is some type of correction. But with the savvy knowledge we hear, gossip offers no protection. Society is me and you, and maybe with some problems, there is nothing that I can do with the news you sell me. I am one of the innocents when you tell me, trying to stay unworldly, if that is how I see me. So when it comes to evil, I say "Shield me!".

Above and Beyond

Above and beyond your Love was a competition, push and shove. They tried to deny me reason, and Love, and I showed up without fear, as I'm leavin', you go above and beyond, so, when we're gone, we stay near. One time you found me low underground, rejecting Love, when I was praying like I don't care and playing like you're not there. But even there, of you, I'll always be fond. Just saying, "I Love you", I go above and beyond.

A Message For You

There is a place beyond expression, for balance, in the Life of a girl who had some talent. Which started in a bad place where she came from. Silenced by some. Faith from not a perfect girl, who shouldn't preach, but who fights for freedom of speech (she confesses). A gift bigger than Life, and almost stopped by all else. If God gives you a message, why would He want you to keep it to yourself?

The Distracted Love

I do Love, but I don't. But I never not Love because I won't. Je ne sais pas exactement qui ils sont.
He gave his Love to me, then retracted, because his True Love was only acted. My biggest mistake was ignored Love. It was distracted.

Protection

I know I exceeded my parents' expectations not because they thought I was Good enough for the world, but because they thought the people of the world were Good enough to deserve me. I'm who I am almost by their promise, their word. Being worthy of each other, we can change the world.

Self

When I talk about myself, sometimes I embellish. They tell me to shut up and tell less. They may say you can't be selfish, but don't let them make you selfless!

Once

Those teachers of Love make a gesture, say Love words, all the while unexpressed Loves in me fester until you've heard. We repeat like a mime until we are face to face with once upon a Time. They told me, "For unrequited Love, there is still a price". But I've ignored those warnings, once or twice. You don't understand the Time in my head, yet my pride, instead, when you're leaving, I say, "Go right ahead!" You do so with style. But you see, I don't Love you just once in a while. You played with me, those pieces of my heart you rearrange, everytime I was trying, I have to ask, "Why does that mood have to change once I'm flying?". To follow intently, those Love songs that know no wrong, and romances, that you convey with sly glances, and that poetry that teaches us when you can't say no to me, (so you call me sappy.) Yes, but once you're happy, you're happy!

Cherish This

Once it was the past, Until the present is how I'm presented at last. And someday, the future will be here, if I'm prepared with what I cherish so dear. 'At Times' is how we categorize minutes, hours and days……..
But 'now' is always!

What To Take

My Life, I am where I've been, and I can Love you depending on when and what you take in. I leave you when parts of me stray. But then parts of me stay. I've worked on honesty. So take my word when I say! And oh! Why must you take away?

There is injustice in the world from all the takers and heart breakers, so that, even the dream makers see Love as unfair, as such. But we can only give so much…..
So take care!

Bravery Chooses Me

After all the men I've Loved, I hate being the same me with a different 'you'. And they force bravery on me for something I'm indifferent to. I find I'm insignificant to the world, with the courage I lack and the courage they flaunt. Why can't I have to be brave for once for something I want?

Love Can Grow

I don't Love politics and worldly things. I Love your look and a kiss. How can I change the world with a little Love like this? '
But when I know who I am by what I Love, you can leave It or take It. You may say my Love is small, in a way, but It's as big as I make It.

Insanity Hurts

If there is no reason to be mean, mean is crazy.

Dare To Think

I think about him. Not because of him.
I think with him. Not for him.
I think like a man when some are scared to think.
I think something bad, and I don't think!
I rest my head on his shoulder when I am tired of thinking.
And all the while, I think for myself, Loving you without blinking.

Dignity Of A Bird

In matters of Life and death, I choose Life (which means I'm trying). And I go down with a ship from a Love that is undying, finding dignity at work on a ship wreck, means, an anchor around my neck couldn't stop me from flying. Each chapter of Life, I turn the page, until the dignity of flying gets me higher in my bird cage.

The Love I Count On

He broke my heart, but that doesn't stop me from sharing Love in a sonnet. 'No faith in me' means nobody else was counting on it. I move on from this faithful Love in rhyming, and by regards, at the bottom of the mountain I'm climbing, I leave It. When I reach the top, they say to me, "You better believe it!"

Love Once

I Love from my gut, a whim and a hunch. I am a product of where I've been. I Loved you once and it ruined my chances for Love again. Everytime I leave you, my heart is staying no matter what the cost. So I remember that old saying, "It is better to have Loved and lost….".

Never Give Up

You were drunk on Love, but now you're sober, looking at Life from underneath the dirt and up above. Just because he broke your heart and you feel Life is over, you don't have to ever give up on Love!

Underdog Artist

If you have an expression you've worked on from the heart, you deserve the whole world to at least consider your art, because the world is a puzzle and your Life proves you own just a part. "We are the least of us", is what you say (and that's a start).

Don't Worry

If all you ever worry about is yourself, you may have something to worry about.

A Message

I feel and feel and feel disdain and the connection we have even though we're apart. I think and think and think about the pain, so for the pleasure, please tell me where to start!! I haven't Lived. I've posed, with too open of a mind and my heart was closed, except for just a little part. So tell me, how does something from my brain produce something from your heart?!

Always A Flaw

You can say you're only human for an excusable flaw and maybe not human for an inexcusable flaw.

Love From Another League

Life isn't a game, yet it was your Love I could have won. They said, "She will break her heart on that one!". You deny it by your kindness, but with every word, it is my heart you fetter. The truth about me is, that with each rejection, I want better and better. So I was attracted by your charm, strong sense of self, mystery and intrigue, knowing, like everybody else, that you were out of my league.

A Question You Ask Yourself

Some people give things up for a Lover so they won't feel alone or distraught. And some of us give up our Lives for someone we don't have, but only have not. If there is a secret in his heart, little or big, I must uncover and dig until I unearth it. Before you give up on anything, you must ask, "Is he really worth it?".

Child At Heart

What is the difference between Loving and wanting? What is the difference of me being proud of you and flaunting? What's the difference between being lost at heart and being a waif? What's the difference in being Loved and knowing for sure you're safe?

Use Of Art

My expressive personality, who I am, I know you see, this broken Love and religion in poetry. An unfair pain in reflective art….. God repairs the brain with His protective heart.

Putting Brains To Use

If you are smart, you'd know how to save you. And if you are wise in your heart, they'll save you!

The Argument

We think we're right, a conversation with our ears closed and a mind made up, because, to our egos, compromise and Truth will always disrupt. They say, "All the bad stuff, she hears and all Good stuff disappears". The more we argue, the less you hear. So, are you spent? So I win the argument?? Of all the points I made though I never made one because in your book, I never won! Everyday we rehearse our verse, until we're ready to converse. But for everyday we say, we have to walk the walk. And I'm ready. So let me know when you'd like to talk!

Love Is Universal

Love is depended on by the powerful, successful, lonely and depressed. Love is depended on by the bereft, by people who have everything, and people who have nothing else left. Love is the goal that makes us cope. It is a shining beacon of hope, and the last straw. In heaven, It is the law, and, in your eyes, It is something I thought I saw, maybe a compromise.

All I Have

As I get older, have I expressed the sappy Love stuff? As we get older, Life is tough. One of my biggest fears is, I wasn't grateful enough. You see someone with nothing and it breaks your heart in halves. I ask, "Won't they receive a blessing?" with all I have.

Singing My Soul Lives, And What Life Gives

I'm supposed to be singing my soul's praise and I'm wailing I Love you, Life, but the Love in my Life is failing and I've made my failure into my study. But of course, I don't blame anybody. Either the world around me is unfair or I'm supposed to be understanding something (I say to my pain) understanding and learning from my heart not from my brain. My brain will probe and prod. It learns to prove there is a God. I dream because I believe in Heaven in my elation. And if it comes True, Heaven isn't just imagination! Not everything is in the skies. And the courage it took to see! I can find pretty much all of it in your eyes when you look at me. Your mind and quick wit are what I am thinking of, but there are many different ways to Love. Saying that, I haven't lied since your hugs and kisses are what I've been denied. I Love you when you don't know and I Love you at your insistence. But I've had to learn to Love you at a greater distance. Remember how the world will push and shove you? When it was that mountain I moved?... That is how I Love you. Some people are out for whatever they can get and we notice the standard they set, with our happy or sad. I want to say, "Look above you!" My examples of Living good or bad, are how I Love you and I'm supposed to be singing my soul's praise and I shout. Well, at the very least, it gives me something to think about.

Travelling Through Life

I go through Life without faith, so I may think but I'm not knowing. Those road blocks say, "You don't know where you are going." On my way a dream of you says, "He makes my spirit soar and my soul, he lifts." Everyday since I was born, those people's Love and scorn, the honor that I've worn was to get somewhere, a place of gifts. Past all this fear, I'm happy simply for getting there. I go through Life care free caring only if I've won, without an adage, like kindness and knowledge too. If you hurt someone, it creates an added baggage, and it will follow you.

The Courage Of Living

I make making Love into taking Love. The more I try to get, the more I die a bit, until you show me the courage of Living. In short, I feel like something's going to give unless I start giving.

When The Poet's Lost

Poems are selfish in a round about way, as the world moves round and round. I just express my Love in a poem as I write it down. I've learned from a Good person, you have to care before you blink and I say, in a poem, "I Love you" in ink, until you recognize me and I've won… instead of just telling someone.

Mortality

Mortality is something I've accepted or I've fought. Either way, to Live is what I'm trying. You are either alive or you are not. There is no such thing as 'dying'. With him, my will to give in my dreams could change reality—But my will to Live doesn't change just because of my mortality.

Obeying What The Fates Say

I will be merry if there's a way and I Love my Life everytime I don't tarry (thinking of what can be taken away) I have a wonderful Life, even without a man, since the Fates say I can. What if "Enjoy!" was their command?

Identity

I Love man, but I've never been a 'Mrs.' (and not even a Ma'am). Neither. I know the way I am but not who I am, so you can't know me either.

Motive

What you are truly after makes or breaks all your attempts and efforts.

Not Proven Yet

Writing about God, for me, is childlike. It is like a kid explaining his or her imaginary friend.......But imagination could turn out to be real.

Finding Someone

Everybody says your dream coming True is out of the question. Well, 'who wouldn't say that?' is the real question.

Vanity

Inevitably, vanity and self admiration lead to overestimating yourself. But you can recognize that!

Life And Death Matter

When it comes to the things you consider "Life and death," how many accomplishments you have won't matter. Only people will.

Worthy?

You won't know you've earned it until you have it.

On The Bright Side

Tough Love is better than no Love.

Music

You use the Love for my mind to mellow me, and, in your heart, there I carelessly find is a melody, right or wrong. Pals go together like the harmony of a song, heard east and west, north and south, as the notes raise like the corners of your mouth to tell me I'm what you chose, and I hear music… a breath that "makes my eyes close"*. And in your eyes, the world, mostly oceans owned by your motion, that never lies. While there is that wave of sound that cries like my soul does to the moon, crashes into me like a tune.

*song of Edith Piaf in movie Saving Private Ryan

His Motive

You didn't like me so you could see how that would strike me, and by your motive, I fell apart. I felt but I didn't know. You didn't want my heart. You wanted to have it, though. Like a damsel in distress, your looks hit me unlike the rest (but mostly), like a locomotive. The real question is, "What was your motive?"

71

Remembering A Prayer

I've survived Life so far, living for dreams and smiles. I've lasted past the tragedies, the tasks and the trials, to realize my dream is far away, from me, in reality, practicality, and the miles (as someone said). My dream is far away from me everywhere (except in my head). Alone now, I'm so scared, I swallow, the more I'm knowing you left, but where are you going, whenever I don't follow? So I rely on my wishes like a religion, to be near... but where? Does anyone hear your prayer? Because I heard you (casually) say, you'll be "here and there".

Making It My Own

Thieves! They don't get it! Don't they know that Love, admiration and respect is the most you can take from people?

Alas

Your eyes, they soothe, and your words are smooth. You break my heart over dinner. My mind is cautious (like a beginner), and you say things that make me raise my glass. Alas, alas!
You say we just don't belong, and there is no doubt for you. So I pour my soul out for you. But you are so strong! I offer myself, another chance to you, and you say, "I'll pass," so I'll speak to myself.... "Alas, alas, alas."

What We Do

Doing what you are allowed to do is the most fun. Out loud, I can call it mine. And doing what you're supposed to do is divine.

For The Future

For the future, I walk toward you now. I walk as easily as God will allow. Everyday is a blessing and a present. My past is a gift for the present. I feel forever when you stare at me. At the same time, I let go of a guarantee, because no future is set as of yet. You ask me, "What comes after?" God help me! It's the laughter. Now is our biggest asset, that I know. For the future, though our Love, hidden from the world, lays our prophecy, that I will always remember you by your philosophy.

Scared

I'm scared of who I am and I'm scared of what I'm not. I'm scared to get away with things and I'm scared that I'll get caught. I'm especially scared of that 'I think you're leaving' thought.
I'm scared I'm weak and I'm scared I'm tough. I'm scared that I'm not scared enough. I'm scared of all those consequences and how I've fared. I'm also scared that I'm so scared!

What My Parents Want For Me

I wish Time would stand still for them, but it won't. They want me to sleep Good, and so I do, but they don't. Yet sometimes this world makes me wake up in a pant. They want me to appreciate youth, and I do, but they can't. All through the Time they helped me believe in myself as a kid, even beyond those things restricted that they forbid, we still say, "I Love you". And when I'm down, and my rewards are long overdue, I ask, "Who wants the world for me now?", but they do.

Belief

How many things, that we truly believe, in the deepest part of our hearts, aren't True?

Someone

I had hoped someone would come to me, not knowing that being someone would come to me.

You, Me, And The World Around Us

The Time of my Life is you, every bit, when it rains. The Time of my Life is lit, but so hard to attain. I want to chase you until you get me (in my heart, you rearrange) in the world you change….. But nobody gets me! I Love you, but I'd have to change my behavior. I don't know you, yet you are my Savior. You think above me and you disrupted me. You Love me, but you won't put up with me.

The Real Reward

You do Good and then look at the world. You'll get rewarded. And if you don't get rewarded, you do Good then look at yourself, you'll get rewarded.

Dustin Pickering

i have a photograph of your soul
which, etched though it is upon my sights,
does not appease my blindness.

and if you ask for trembling you will see
my despair at your absence and simple defiance.

Antigone's last touch will crawl from your eye
into my senselessness and the ensuing pleasures of loss.

you aren't what i said in the original black book.

fiery winter woman

in the blaze of the saddle of snow
the crux of all unknown variables
will anger the void, stirring compromise.

and all the struggle of fear
within the empty illusions of childhood's soul
will open the drawers of the bedlam
encasing the insolence of monopolized wind

bring the energy to itself:
rage and faith
occupy the end of time

when you examine your greatest fear
foe of man appears
thoughts disappear
you hang from one hand to another—
seeking only the grievances you have adorned
with paper and purple curtain.

grief does not stand [neither sit nor play]

I swim to the constant arrival of my pleasures
by the time dawn escapes my lips—
you are still there in the hapless nothingness
of my intentions

and with everything you wish
comes this dream of flaw and fast hopes
which die in the light before leaves crisp
and cankerworms devour the remnants of your life

a poem merely grasps the narrow function—
holding to the rivers of Seeming
all possible pastimes are unspoken.

the exegesis of compassion
flunked by dogs of the worst day

if anything was to come from this...
if anything. your mind is a shallow pool.

when the categories drop your system of solace
black thought tyrannizes your purposeful display.

we have awakened our own dominance
like animals of war or love—
now that you have devised synonyms from my games
I can call your desperation from its intimacy
expunge your dreams from the worrisome dust

when you climb back from the wounds of your night vision
the dolls speak to your hearts tied intricately.

complex knots only clutter the whole sign language
of this destiny
a ship will come sooner if you inundate the lies

if I eat or take this wafer—oblivion, sound—
I must forgive my past,
let it haunt the soul of my lost hands;
we know that time is taking too long.
breadth of night keeps the sayings of dreamers
in the broken cups
in the lost clouds of one's own hiddenness

I thicken my own gravity
approaching the lines of charcoal drawn
against the wind—

doesn't this fascinate the world turning
 from its own remembrances—
thoughts no longer count.
they are empty pastimes.

folds in the crying distance
like cyanide from Loki's heart
strained by strangers of fictitious brain

the hymns of the light
darken when his angel opens the flesh
like a hook saving the fish from water.

when thought is kept mercifully
by the dying, who darken the page
unlike the sunshine faith feelings
tar hardens the remaining beauty
mangled and morphing from gratitude
to conspicuous hate

earth is forgotten lust—pangs of Nirvana
stored against the shallow waste of defiance.
I call the answer to our predicament
and internal demise.

the clock strikes favorable time—
once of twice it is beaten from the sky
where golden rains and silver faces
placate the dead. again there is no harm to them.

how do you expect to unravel
these solemn mysteries
when your only mind
is set to dominate and not cast away?

a bone is broken is field of flies.
they never come to me, waiting,
hoping for the dismal satisfaction
of the ghosts.

turn the door handle—
its moth-like solemnity baffles the imagination.
are we the only beings conscious of prey?
hand me the silence of your forgotten flames.
darken this pasture with an old token of strife.

memories are not courted by their faith.
what you think you remember
is an amalgamation of your own fantasies
tied and tripped to the watch of the republic.

listen to the things of the dream.
an ear for the sanctity of hollowness
as emptiness contemptuously
cries the last instance of your epoch.

truth is a scourge to all mortality
waiting in the dusk of all game—
thinking again of taking what does not belong
and leaving it for the shadows of complicit judgment.

now if you know the future from this dotted line
do not think to sign—faith blisters the bleeding hearts.

I will not resurrect your truly demolished ruin
until you renounce toil and timelessness.

hence the rivers of judgment cleanse the barter
of your soul for the truth—but only *they* know.

when I hear the compulsions of horror
through facades where the beaten leave their trials
I know a stone reckons, trembling in the central grid.

how we don't see with eyes bandaged by nurses
of the flagship where we haunt an agnostic rattle
of bones and blown fists of wind.
from what were we born but yearned undecided
by this contest of wills?

a thought sanctimonious in its own keeping—
demise is waiting, once, but it will not come again.

Blake withstood your heart, canceled by the rain and coal
flung to the damnations—once the mystery is solved.

your own whimsical notions are solvent
to perplexed deviance.

but does the reign hold the horse in brutal subjugation…
or does the starlit castanet bleakly resolve our fear?

who can taste so much this entranced ardor of Nature?

purple drifts into my coffee, feeling guilt for the future
which will announce itself like a dismal curve
never reaching its destination.

only the stars know what is to come. lift the wings of thought!
pale and posthumous glory spent,
if only your eyes were wicked enough.
I climb the only remaining day in our wasted fear.
dark and attentive to the slights we endured,
a god reaches into the folds of coupling
we draw through one another.

love is only a circle brought to justice.

when beauty stops at the door, waiting to know intentions
from the embodied past—
how and when do blind forces resign from your eyes?

as I implode in the secrecy of god's twisted regions—
eyes will face like a shepherd, this stark entity remaining flat.
plateau of this starving body,

yet how can we own the land of our seeking?

between the dark and deadly
after the art and animosity
comes the drifters singing,
singing the deep song.

made from tendencies unknown, unheard,
unspoken: restitution knows its place.

anything can bleed in higher terms.

Some poems from Dustin Pickering's section are from "Ghosts at the Bridges of My Soul," poems which placed in the top 100 longlist in the erbacce prize of over 12,500 entries in 2021.

Dory Williams is a 45 year old Texan who has been writing poetry for 27 years. She loves movies and taking care of animals. Dory studied as an English major at the University of Texas- Austin. Recently she has been working toward health, independence, an enlightened view of Life and the poetry that reflects it. Publications include: Sechiisland's International Library (in Rio Claro, Brazil) Lone Stars Magazine (out of San Antonio, Texas) and Blue Moon Poetry (out of NC). She has also been reviewed by DJ Tyrer of Essex, UK and Andy Robson of "Krax Magazine" of Yorkshire, England.

Dustin Pickering is founder of Transcendent Zero Press and founding editor of *Harbinger Asylum*. He has contributed writing to *Huffington Post*, *Café Dissensus Everyday*, *The Statesman* (India), *Journal of Liberty and International Affairs*, *Colorado Review*, *World Literature Today*, and several other publications. He is a Pushcart and Best of the Net nominee.

www.ingramcontent.com/pod-product-compliance
Lightning Source LLC
Chambersburg PA
CBHW060400050426
42449CB00009B/1831